Beauty Within the Chaos

Lynsey Austin

Presentation by *BookLeaf Publishing*

Web: www.bookleafpub.com

E-mail: info@bookleafpub.com

ISBN: 9789358317947

First edition 2023

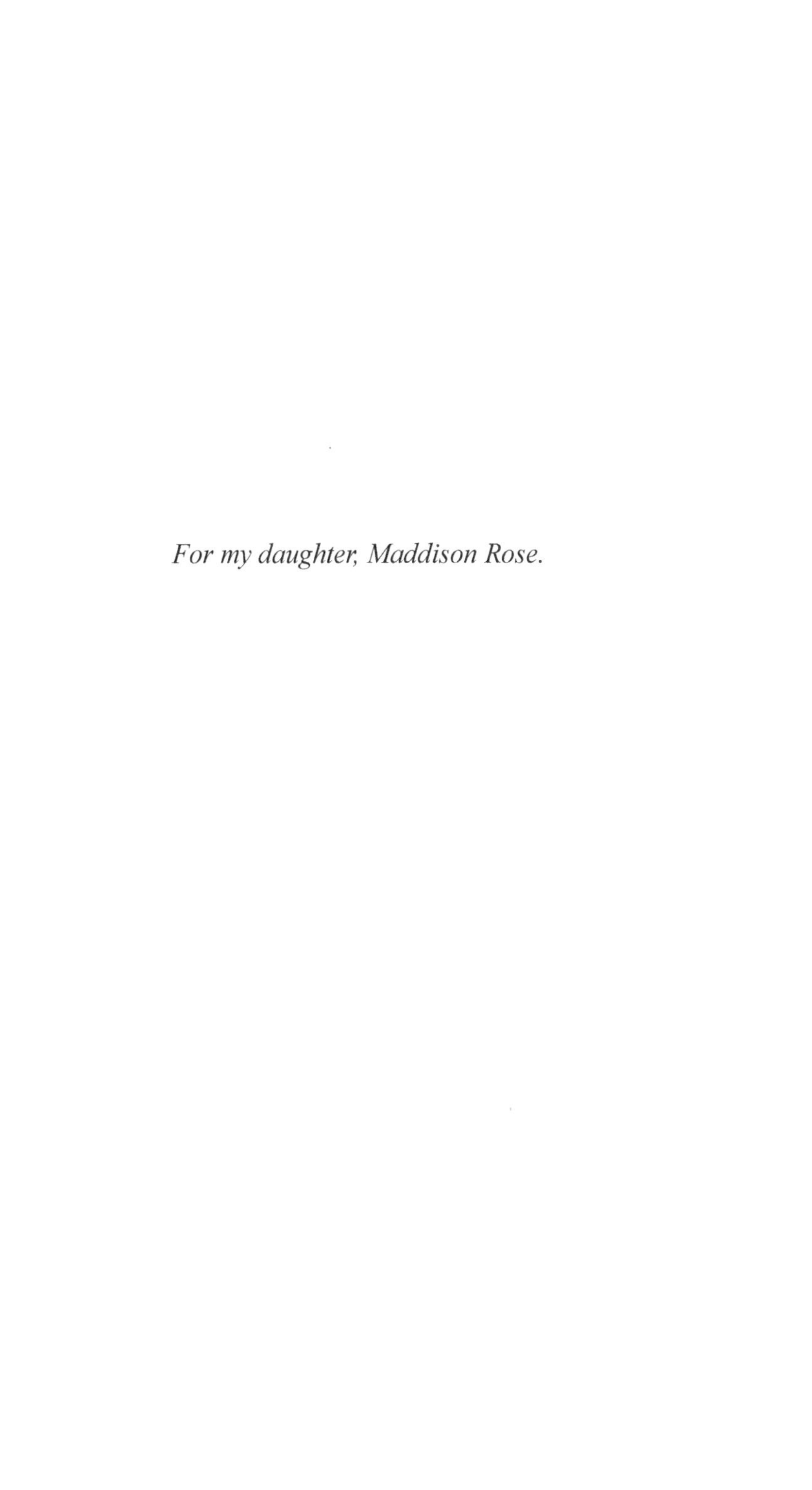

For my daughter, Maddison Rose.

Grass

The grass is not greener on the other side.
Today I got myself worked up into such anger
and stress. I cried.
The grass won't glow greener by standing aside.
Some parts of me are kept concealed, some
might say I lied.
Your grass won't glow greener staring at your
peers.
I get blamed for their lack of action; they should
confront their own fears.
There is no grass where I am standing.

My Alter Ego

I feel them staring at me.
I feel that hungry, dominant gaze.
When they look, what do they truly see?
Every inch of me feels flawed, exposed, seen.

Beneath the beauty, the material, the smile
I cover up my pain, I am adamant it must hide.
Their phone to hand, my number they dial.
When that call shows up, my alter ego is
revealed.

I listen as they touch themselves, the closer they
get, the louder they sound.
The words, phrases, sighs. The encouragement
flows so easily now.
Every second, every minute, rounds up to the
next pound.
The call ends, but for me, the feelings linger.

Sometimes, quite rarely, you'll get caught out.
The caller will be refreshing, kind, arousing.
This work, I call a career, I am devout.
I want their calls, want their money, need their
desire.

Every penny ties up my self-worth.

The quiet days drag, my confidence falters.
Yet I am never surprised by size, beauty nor
girth.
What will surprise me, the shock, the rejection
once my beauty dries up.
Where then, does my alter ego go?

The Dominatrix

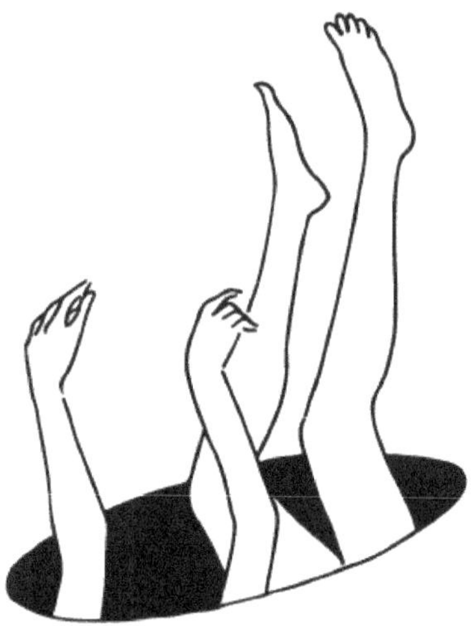

To have power or influence over someone.
To have sense of self-control undone.
To cause embarrassment or shame.
The deepest form of mind control, that is my
aim.

I pull out my whip and roll straight in with
flogging,
Despite how harsh, pain gets them throbbing.
My goal is to completely and utterly dominate,
And in return for this, they financially
compensate.

I will belittle and shame, anyone else would be
sobbing,
To those that are vanilla, the experience would
be shocking.
The client enjoys it, his member grows greedy,
I ramp up my torture, this one is needy.

Both sexual and mental, the control I take.
In a world full of decisions, in this sanctuary,
only I can make.
Some may judge this world and attach shame.
Enter the kink world, you'll realise this is tame.

PVC, leather, whips and toys I have plenty.
The aim of the session is to have mind and balls
empty.
I push boundaries until they break,
Inflict pain until they ache.

Each moment they devour,
When I take the power.
The human mind, how it does fascinate.
I do not procrastinate.
My role is to dominate.

Gratitude

In a world full of negativity,
The joy we must find.
In every moment of pain and darkness,
We must encourage happiness to glow inside.

I discovered the law of attraction,
And embraced it into every part of my life.
I searched for the positive in every moment.
I found it. I found warmth amongst the strife.

I exude gratitude.
I deeply and utterly appreciate even the smallest
of joy.
In moments I would have previously
overlooked.
I am hopeful, my eyes are wide, like a child with
a new toy.

You attract what you focus on.
My life began to change.
I noticed a flick of a switch in my mindset.
And the miraculous moments flowed within
range.

I reached out, embraced them.
That is when I came to realise,

Since this experience has begun,
My life, I own, I personalise.

I love, experience and live more deeply.
In return, the universe sends me more blessings.
I receive, embrace and devour every joyous
moment.
The way I live, I love. I am no longer left
stressing.

Compare Me Not

In my own home
Security
Mentally and physically.

When I am all alone
Confidence
In my abilities and my appearance.

Cast me into a social setting.
Weakness.
I compare myself to others.

They are more beautiful than me.
Their outfit looks better than mine.
They have a lifestyle and income which offers
them more.

I feel
Deflated
Drained
Collapsed

I falter when surrounded by comparison.
My strengths fade into a void.
I have never felt more alone than when I am
surrounded by people.

Strangers who make me feel strange.

Is this social anxiety?
Or simply a lack in my own confidence?

It is not their intention.
They are kind.
My mind is not.

Is it worth it?

The Little Crystal Collection

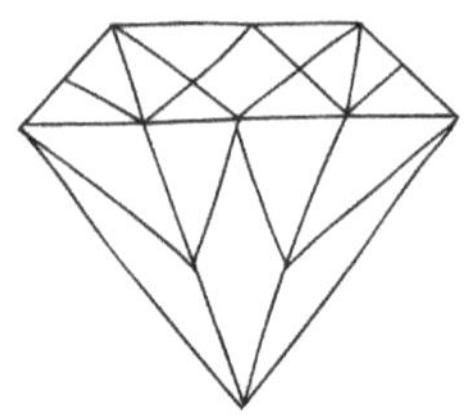

I've got candles and crystals a-plenty,
Rose Quartz of all kinds, yet want more.
Green crystals to eradicate the envy,
And Hagstones found down by the shore.
Yet there's only one I carry with me everywhere,
It gets kept in my bra all day.
This on in particular, it's rare.
My go to crystal; Jade!
In distressing situations, it calms the mind,
Has an energy and presence of its own.
Brings luck and wealth of all kinds,
So many benefits in such a small stone.
And if someone talks and takes a rude tone,
Grab it, aim for them, and throw!

I Run

I run, it makes me strong.
I can keep pace with my child.
When we dance and make up a song.

I run, it brings me peace.
Calm and serene, I hear barely a noise,
Aside from the birds and the breeze.

I run, it keeps me slim.
It is what the media wants,
I need something to keep me trim.

I run, it clears my mind.
All the chaos disappears,
The calm is what I find.

I run, I feel free.
I can go wherever I wish,
Past the meadows, the parks, the sea.

I run.
I run away.

Journey

My mind blurs and feelings emerge.
A unique calm surrounds me.
The tension dispersed; I was on the verge.
But it's gone.

Materials feel different somehow.
My sheets, heavy yet comforting.
I feel cool yet a sweat on my brow.
I am safe and warm.

Every move I make I can hear—
The blood pumping fast through my veins,
It sounds so distant, but it is so near.
My body is a song.

This room I fill daily looks different.
Objects swirl into colour,
It surrounds me, engulfs me, is potent.
Everything merges into one.

The narcotics wear off.
The heaviness returns.
Where is the rest? I will devour in a quaff.
But it's gone.

The Bar

She sits at the bar,
It's quiet for a Saturday.
Waiting for her friend, she claims she's not far,
She sits and waits anxiously.
Pretending to scroll her phone.
Avoiding the male gaze.
Being watched makes her feel alone.
Every minute passes like days.
She wants another drink,
The bartender eyes her.
What must people think?
She opens her mouth, her words are a slur.
A male staring gets her attention.
He approaches with a smile and a wink.
She knows exactly his intention.
Remaining passive and polite, she sips her drink.
His conversation makes no sense.
She barely responds.
Watching the clock in suspense.
The men just see an attractive, young blonde.
She has now had enough,
To the ladies she goes.
Has she been stood up?
Only her friend knows.
She gives her a call.
Straight to voicemail.

How long should she wait in this stall?
Staring at every tile, every detail.
That's when she hears it.
The laugh, so infectious and loud.
She heads back down in a flit.
Finally, there she is, sitting confident and proud.
The nerves disappear.
Her head is suddenly clear.
Now, time for a good time, and another beer.

Lost in Fog

The stark reality strikes like a hot iron
One moment, frozen in time
Will never be forgotten.
A loss like no other.
The laughter and smiles disperse.
The sadness surrounds and suffocates me.
Covering me like a blanket.
Inescapable. I can't breathe.
My world has been swiped from beneath me,
Every minute feels empty
Consumed by mundane sadness,
All track of time lost.
I move through time lifeless,
No spark left in my eyes.
No motive or desire left within me.
A part of my soul was stolen from me.
This darkness engulfs and cradles me.
It is the fog that surrounds my every move and
thought.
I don't want to leave this dark cocoon.
This sadness starts to feel familiar.
I don't want to move on in my life without you.
I want to stay consumed in this fog,
Moving on means accepting you are no longer
here.
Everything reminds me of you;

The Robins that appear at my back door,
The notebook with your name on,
The shirt I wore when I last saw you.
How can I move through this fog when you left
so much behind?
Only an empty life consumed by fog remains.

Still Trying to Meet a Man...

I am trying to meet a man,
I created a foolproof plan.
I will download all the apps,
Change my radius on the maps,
Then drive round the wealthy towns in laps.

Autumn

Orange and brown, fading from green.
The leaves crunch beneath my feet,
Tree branches bare and seen.
The temperature is dropping, I'm craving the
heat.

The air carries a cleansing breeze,
Rain falls more often, the coolness shocks,
Deep in your chest, every breath is a wheeze.
A witch in my street! On my door she knocks.

I open my door 'trick or treat!'
Loaded with sweets, she skips back up the path,
Within the hour, I had been cleaned out by the
street.
Up the stairs I go for a steamy hot bath.

My favourite place to be, a book in my hand,
Shut off from the world, in my own little land.

Have I Got Covid?

Have I got Covid?
I have a cough,
I have been up all night,
I want this barking to stop.

Have I got Covid?
My chest feels heavy,
Every breath is an effort.
I don't feel too healthy.

Have I got Covid?
My body aches all over.
Every moment is painful.
I know I'm such a moaner.

Have I got Covid?
My temperature is high.
I have come out in cold sweats,
I just want to cry.

Have I got Covid?
Everyone avoids me.
They don't want to catch it.
What I would give, to be germ free.

Have I got Covid?
The test says negative,
Though everyone now avoids me,
Friends, colleagues and relatives.

My Cat, Bobby

His eyes, pupils dilated—
Look into me like he reads my soul.
His black and white coat—
Thick, silky, the softest you ever felt.
His white patches are always bright and
perfectly clean.
He disappears at night—
Always returning, routinely, at sunrise.
Crying for food, dramatizing in response to my
words.
Light on his feet with such grace.
Neither human nor dog can move swift like him.
His hearing—supernatural.
He hears my car rattle down the road from
streets away.

Sitting, waiting for me.
In tune with my emotions
Whether sad or poor.
He comforts me with his presence and purring.
People—they say, 'cats are selfish'(!)
They just don't understand them.
Cats don't need mollycoddling.
And those that need to be needed—
Are better off with a dog!

Single Parenthood

I raise her all alone.
In this apartment we call home.
Despite being 29 years younger—
She is my mini me, I love her.

The chaos of juggling all on my own—
Is a struggle, harder than you'll ever know.
But watching her grow makes it worth it.
I get these moments on my own, they are
perfect.

We are a team, for us it works.
Life through a four-year-old's eyes has its perks,
I slow down and absorb every moment.
It's underrated, this whole 'being a single
parent.'

Other parents may look and feel sorry for you.
I feel sorry for them, sharing a child between
two.
They don't need to pity me, we are more than
just fine,
Our life is full of love and laughter, the pity, it's
all mine.

Don't ever judge a parent on their own.
Mind your own business, the truth you'll never
know.

Toxic Media

Who do we believe?
The media is confusing,
It traps our mind,
Leaves us to believe stuff of all kinds.

Women's bodies are ridiculed
By both men and women
Yet the male form takes no scrutiny,
We let it go on, foolishly.

They take pictures of celebrities
And fabricate their own stories.
We believe it and gossip,
Even when we know, it is clearly a fib.

Their take on the pandemic
Made the vulnerable terrified.
How do we let them get away with it?
Most of their work, no better than clickbait.

Social media thrives on it
A problem alone that consumes us.
I will break free from the habit.
Just mindless scrolling on gadgets.

I need to break this addiction,
Like most, it is bad for you.
The relationship is toxic,
An addiction not based on logic.

Love or Lust?

Love or lust?
A desire to touch,
To reach out, hold them close,
Explore every inch of them, your crush.

Love or lust?
They consume all your thoughts.
Playing out scenarios you desire,
Involving them in life choices of all sorts.

Love or lust?
Their opinions matter the most,
No care for what others think.
What your lover chooses, is the option that goes.

Love or lust?
Delicate, eye-watering beauty,
I could gaze at them forever.
Like I was made for them to adore them my
duty.

Love or lust?
They have such focus and drive,
It inspires and lifts me.
It is contagious, resulting—for better things I
strive.

Love or lust?
I feel safe with them around.
A bubble of security I have never felt,
I want to stay forever, in this bubble please keep
me bound.

Love or lust?
I want them to penetrate every corner of my life,
Explore everything that has built me,
Meet every parent, sibling, cousin, and even
their wife.

Love or lust?
In this moment it feels like the former.
It could develop into more, or on the flipside
trauma.
Chaotic confusion, how is this normal?

Cold Walk Home

Slowly, trudging through the leaves
Hiding my fingers in my sleeves.
The cold is sharp, my nose shines red,
Wind whipping my hair around my head.
The sun sets early, the nights are long,
An urge to hide in bed is strong.
I wonder how the magpies feel,
No central heating for them to steal.
It starts to rain and soaks me through
Every part of me soggy, even through my shoe.
The cold, the wet, I feel it deep,
Right down to my bones—it starts to seep.
I start walking faster, I want to be home.
Moving my feet so fast across the stone,

Then finally, I reach the door.
Just as the rain really starts to pour.
I turn the key and step inside,
For the rest of the night, this is where I will hide.

Soulful Stars

When I look up into the sky,
At home, in bed, staring up as I lie.
The night is clear, there is so much to see
Oh how it must feel, to be a star floating free.
I have a belief that within these stars,
Contained are memories that could heal my
scars.
Our loved ones past, can watch and glow,
As we carry on life down far below.
Their souls held and preserved up high
Waiting for us to say goodbye.
And when it's our time, we will join them too.
As a sparkling star, shining bright, brand new.

Generational Trauma

Our childhoods are formed by our mum and dad.
I reflect on mine, and it makes me sad.
My parents separated at a young age,
For most of their relationship, not on the same
page.
My mum quickly moved onto someone new.
Two families merged; he had kids too.
My mum moved on without healing,
Her existing trauma, erupting and feeling.
Needless to say, her relationship was toxic.
The effect it left on me was emotionally chronic.
My needs as a child were rarely met,
How she let this happen, I will just never get.
The generational trauma stops right here!

I'll never put my child through that, and I am
making it clear!
My relationship with both mum and dad is still
strained,
Just thinking about it leaves me emotionally
drained.
My promise to my child is I will strive to be
better.
Whenever she needs me, I'll be present to help
her.
I am healing my wounds through my own
version of parenting.
Every day gets easier, heart and mind are
strengthening.

Cash Flow

Money doesn't grow on trees,
Nor does it just appear.
But without it, life can be a squeeze,
And you can end up with a backlog of arrears.
I work so hard to bring in the dough,
And spend it ever so fast.
My bank account looks way too low,
Payday seems so long ago in the past.
Money won't make you happy; they say,
And with it more problems come.
But I'd have one less problem with all my bills paid,
And a Merc with leather seats for my bum!

Constellation

High up in the sky you shine
In the light of the moon you
Flourish. It does not end, time
Rolls on, the seconds are few.
What I would do to gain more,
More nights under the stars
What has my life get in store
How much more time will now pass?

Secrets

Secrets. We all have them.
Some are hidden so deep they become us.
Hers are hidden beneath her femme.
Her beauty and seduction rise, causing other
issues to hush.
That's how she keeps them hidden.
Distraction is her greatest skill.
By seduction that will leave you smitten.
She is as addictive as a pill.
You will never unlock the truth.
She is far too dangerous to allow it.
Don't bother attempting to snoop.
You are already her next target.

Notebook

Crisp new page of white.
Ready for me to fill with shite.
Diary entries, revision notes, maybe a story.
Some written elegant, some more gory.
But as I look at this empty page
My mind is blank, I panic in the bright light of
the stage.
The urge to fill it, complete it, drives me.
But God how intimidating it can be.
Entirely confident yet totally insecure,
Who intends to read my words, raw and pure.
One day they will take it and decide.
'This notebook must be read, the rantings of her
mind!'

My Rose

The world revolves around her,
Every decision I make, daily.
From the moment she arrived,
She will forever be my baby.

It's a common turn of phrase,
A child's love is like no other.
But for me it runs much deeper,
That moment I became a Mother.

Before her, life lacked purpose.
Trapped in my mind and not the moment.
Now everything has changed,
That motherly love is potent.

Some days can be a struggle,
Balancing everything alone.
No other adults for company,
Only the words across my phone.

Before she arrived, I lacked a family.
I also lacked a career.
Oh, how life took such a turn,
The moment she did appear.

Generational patterns broken
Toxic friendships hit their limit
I have never felt so liberated,
No one around me can break my spirit.

In my life I now have beauty,
In physical and mental form.
This love that I am blessed with,
Can guide me through any storm.

The world revolves around us,
Every decision I make, daily.
Through every single storm,
I will guide you through to safety.

Just Hold My Hand

Holding hands not holding heart,
Going through the motions, not feeling it from
the start.
'He is good for you,' they say,
They are right of course, but my mind starts to
stray.
He is loving, kind and treats me with respect,
My mind is set to appreciate but my heart wants
to reject.
He wants to see me all the time,
But I feel like a fraud committing a crime.
I want to like him, want to love him.
My stubborn heart won't have it, she engages in
sin.
I try my hardest to force a connection,
But his open-heart forces me in the opposite
direction.
I don't love him, but he must love me,
To be as patient as he has shown himself to be.
Do I keep trying, keep convincing myself?
Or end it, protecting my mental health?
I need to choose, seek real love or be smart?

In the meantime, I'll be holding his hand, but never his heart.